CW00410029

ROUTE 66

OPEN ROAD FOR PROMISELAND

John Powls – Poems

*To Roger
with my best wishes
John Powls
Jan 2017*

Carol Ballenger – Images

ALSTAR

With affection, for The Mother Road and all her children
JP

For the photographic pioneers of the Wild West whose legacy continues to inspire.
CB

Acknowledgements

We wish to thank Simon Butler and Sharon O'Inn at Halsgrove and Graham Hodgson for their help in the production of this book and Google for permission to include images made using Google Earth and Street View.

First published in Great Britain in 2016

Copyright © John Powls - Poems 2016
Copyright © Carol Ballenger - Images 2016

Attribution
all images © 2016 Google except:
© 2015 Google pp 11, 18, 43, 77
© 2016 Google, Image Landsat pp 8, 9, 28, 35, 60, 61, 71, 73,
      75, 82
© 2015 Google, Image Landsat p 7
© 2016 Google, © 2016 INEGI pp 23, 26, 29, 38, 40, 85, 87, 95
© 2015 Google, © 2015 INEGI p 91

All rights reserved. No part of this publication may be reproduced, stored in a retrieval system, or transmitted in any form or by any means without the prior permission of the copyright holder.

British Library Cataloguing-in-Publication Data
A CIP record for this title is available from the British Library

ISBN 978 1 906690 64 9

HALSTAR
Halsgrove House,
Ryelands Business Park,
Bagley Road, Wellington, Somerset TA21 9PZ
Tel: 01823 653777   Fax: 01823 216796
email: sales@halsgrove.com

Part of the Halsgrove group of companies.
Information on all Halsgrove titles is available at: www.halsgrove.com

Printed in China by Everbest Printing Investment Ltd

'Many a trip continues long after movement in time and space have ceased'
John Steinbeck   Travels With Charley: In Search of America

'We had longer ways to go. But no matter, the road is life'
Jack Kerouac   On The Road

*'Leading me wherever I choose. You express me better than
I can express myself – more to me than my poem.'*
Walt Whitman   The Open Road

*'I, too, was rolling effortlessly along, turning the windshield into a
movie screen in which I, the viewer, did the moving while the subject
held still. That was the temptation of the American highway.'*
John Least Heat-Moon   Blue Highway

The Poems

I had long had the ambition to produce poetry inspired by the landscape of the USA to which I was drawn from childhood by movies, music and by the work of Walt Whitman, John Steinbeck and Jack Kerouac - a fascination only heightened by visits to the country.

That aspiration became centred on Route 66 - the iconic 'Mother Road' and an enduring symbol of Americana with its hinterland of iconography and imagination as vast as its geography.

To meet that exciting artistic challenge, I needed immersion and to get the trip – physically and poetically – trading stories along the way. So, in September 2014, after many enjoyable months of research, planning and organising, I drove 'Main Street USA' solo, 'more than two thousand miles all the way' from Chicago to the California coast over three weeks.

'Route 66 - open road for promiseland' is my narrative sequence of poems inspired by that journey through the landscape and experience of the American road trip.

A landscape poet inspired by the Romantic tradition, I also engage with wide cultural influences and develop my particular heritage of language with its North East of England roots.

As a result, my poems feature alliteration, compression, comparison, contrast and compound words with strong themes and imagery rooted in legend, landscape and weather that command attention – another attraction for me of Route 66 as a subject.

I aim to achieve freshness and focus in innovative realisation of my ideas on the page and am stimulated by the interplay of anticipation, memory and experience in doing so.

For this road trip project, employing my long established way of working, I made notes of words, phrases, ideas and feelings along the way and as part of my evening review of each day on the road or in each stopover location.

The poems were initiated from those many fragments, edited on my return to the UK, and then were formed, crafted and finished over a two year period, fitting within my chosen narrative style and framework and illuminating my key impressions.

That process included exchanging with Carol Ballenger as she produced images in response to my poems and development through a number of solo readings and performances with Carol and other poets and musicians.

I have collaborated with Carol on many projects for over twenty years and was hugely pleased when I saw the results of the exciting approach she was taking. I was very grateful that she then agreed to provide images for this book that work with my poems in an innovative and distinctive joint approach to the American road trip.

John Powls

The Images

Google Earth and Street View have replaced my cameras for this project. I have never actually been on Route 66, even though I grew up in America, but I am pleased to have made and documented my virtual journey from Chicago to California.

For over 30 years I have been photographing the landscape, rural and urban, making black and white darkroom prints, moving to colour, then using a digital camera and Photoshop. Working with Google Earth has been a continuing development in my photographic practice and enabled me to use conventional photographic skills in a new context. Developed in 2007, Google Street View sees all and is non-selective. Providing a rich and unlimited amount of material to explore, its accessibility has inspired many artists who are using it to document the world.

I began working with satellite images that showed the terrain crossed by Route 66. In response to John's poems I also used Street View to travel along the road, looking for subjects just as if I had a camera. The quality of the images varies considerably depending on the location, but I decided to retain many of the quirks, including blurred signs and faces and image artefacts, as these elements are inherent in the original capture. Photoshop was used to crop, make adjustments to contrast and colour, and apply filters to make an image I felt complemented a particular poem. Many images through colour and texture are reminiscent of historic postcards of Route 66.

The history of landscape photography is integrally linked to the American West. William Henry Jackson, Timothy O'Sullivan and Carleton Watkins travelled west in the 1860s to document objectively the terrain and early settlements. The 20th century saw the development of the medium through the work of photographers such as Ansel Adams, whose pioneering darkroom techniques and richly detailed prints were to transform ideas about landscape photography and how we looked at the environment. William Eggleston showed how colour could be an important element in its own right and that anything could be subject matter for a photograph. He said, "I had this notion of what I called a democratic way of looking around, that nothing is more or less important." This of course ties in with the all-encompassing nature of Street View. In 1975 Robert Adams showed work in a groundbreaking exhibition called "New Topographics" which revealed a strange beauty in banal subjects presented in a detached way. More recently in 2011 Doug Rickard, using Google Street View, published a series of photographs of neglected neighbourhoods called "A New American Picture".

My work has been inspired by this photographic legacy, the poems of John Powls and, above all, the great American landscape of Route 66.

Carol Ballenger

The Prospect: Lucy Is Heading Home To Chicago
Chicago, Illinois

So it turns out
Lucy is heading home
To Chicago
And I am set
For the start of 66

Single seat
Algorithm allocation
Brought us close
But implied etiquette
Of no algorhyme
Or reason meant
Silence settled
With the first
Flipped down tray
And we didn't
Trade our stories
Until the mercifully
Slick stack
Over O'Hare

In the way
Of these things
By the time
We've circled

Down to tarmac
Wheelsmoke spirals
We know some chapters
And a few verses

She returning to family
From her trip of a lifetime
And I about to start mine
Both excited at
The Prospect

I have a hunch
This is the first
Time of many
I will trade
My edited story
With other travellers
And territorials
Over days and distances
To come
Embellished
By every experience

It is far from
The first time

I have told it
To myself
In prospect
Ambition long held
But at last
I am in
Ruthless search
Of my theme

Letting the road
Lead me
Where I chose
It's the getting there
And
The getting there
Getting the trip
In the car
That is the
Moving figure
That most revealed
Created and changed
The ground it crossed

Lucy listens
And proffers herstory

The closeness
Only permitted by
These one time
Briefest encounters

That's the point too

And she raises
The prospect
Of Whitman
Steinbeck and Kerouac
And Mother Road
To follow
With no option
But to make
Your own way

By the time we reach
Gate goodbyes
And good lucks
I am good and ready
To go solo
I realise

O'Hare Airport, Chicago
41° 58' 38.10" N
87° 54' 19.35" W

O'Hare Airport, Chicago
41° 58' 55.30" N
87° 54' 44.82" W

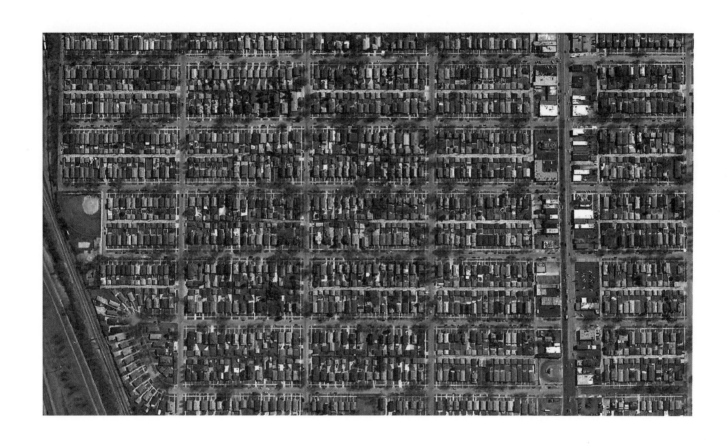

Chicago
41° 47' 46.24" N
87° 47' 47.38" W

Robert Johnson Blues
Chicago, Illinois

America
Beats on it
From all sides
Being the most
American
Chicago beats
Right back

Midwest and Michigan
Moulded
Wind whipped
Intense vitality
And energy
The hub
The heart
The destination
The wild onion
The big shoulders

Exciting
City of cycles
Clean corrupt
Constant renewal
Blocks of steel
And concrete
Towering achievements

Stand the
Phantom fields
Tamed and shackled
And woods
Long piled
Buildings
And blocks
Jackscrewed
Streams descended
To pipe and
Sewers vein
The skin
Of tarmacadam

Drawn and destined
For this town
You found
Your voice, your beat
At that crossroads
Set the soundtrack
For a century
Your songs
Sung by city birds
At dead of night
Under electric stars

Inspired
In the dawning
Down from
The Drake above
The Gold Coast
I fingerscribe
A heart
In the wet sand
Making an impression
In the way
I want
The word

South of Navy Pier
In from Lakeshore
Grant Park green
Across Michigan
Turn right
On red
Adams runs due west
Prairie
Wind measures
Its length

Morning sun
At my back

Rising rays slice
Sixty-six
Straight start
Skyscrapers
Set like standing stones

Adams/Wabash
L station
Lintels
The route
open road for promiseland

This is where
It all began

Ideas have fetches
Great journeys
Ending over horizons
Now imagined

I beat a path

House of Blues, Chicago
41° 53' 17.36" N
87° 37' 45.72" W

Angel Goes To Pontiac
Atlanta, Illinois

By name, narrative
And natural beauty
Angel
Of Atlanta IL
Serves Palms Grill
Blue Plate Specials
Pie and coffee
And charm
To the old man river
Of Route 66ers
Rolling through
En route Missouri
Their stories arc

Though the
Table switched
Greyhound
Stop light
No longer calls
The sleek
And silver bus

Her Homecoming
Radiance, innocent
Is its own attraction
For the now
Not so sleek
But just as silver

Her experience
County circumscribed
She speaks volumes
For Logan's
Welcoming spirit
Says more than
Any mural can
And stops
Muffler Man's
Attempt to
Create an impression
Through size and age
And sheer
Hot doggedness

What use
Would an Angel
Have for
A passport
But oh, will your
Stories arc
Spread your wings
And take you to a
Vicarious world
That needs your grace

Or to Pontiac
At least

The just passing through
Will always come to you

Palms Grill, Atlanta
40° 15' 37.98" N
89° 13' 53.36" W

Muffler Man, Atlanta
40° 15' 38.86" N
89° 13' 53.58" W

Grain Elevators, Elkhart
40° 1' 20.35" N
89° 28' 53.93" W

The Opening Chapters
Illinois and Missouri

From Pontiac
And Atlanta
Across
Illinois and Missouri
I trace
Byway 66
Where its remains
Are available
Uninterrred by Interstates
55 and 44
Lesser numbers

Once bypassed
By more than
New tarmac
Designed for
Distance and speed
Not knowing
Out of sight
Mind and discourse
But now
Reawakening
With its artefacts
Signs and signals
Typography and tin

Pasttowns and
Presentcities
Encounters with
Landscape and history
Interpreted with their
Stories being written
Re-interpreted
From changing
Perspectives
The America experiment
Remains a work
In progress

Character emerges
From outlines
As the narrative
Is framed
In its opening
Chapters

Waypoints
As my journey
Hits its stride

What is in a name
Most everything
Apparently

Springfield IL
Lincolntown
Cozy Dog Drive In
And Shea Gas station

Across the Mississippi
At St Louis
Riverboats
Gateway Arch
Sweetie Pie and soulfood

Meramec, Ozarks and
Mark Twainery

Springfield MO
Victorian old town
Storytrading on
The veranda of
Walnut Street Inn
Dining at Gilardi
In its own
Market garden

Sixty six
Clips Kansas
Breaks Missouri
Into Oklahoma

And me
Into the rhythm
Of the road
As I hit the highway
Past Tulsa

When my mind
Is free
Words
Move in and
Move me on
Beginning to appreciate
What it takes
To get the trip
And the plains
In plain
View

And the clean
Expectant pages

Main Street, Pontiac
40° 52' 49.69" N
88° 37' 42.71" W

Cozy Dog Drive In, Springfield
39° 45' 44.69" N
89° 38' 54.11" W

Soulsby's Service Station, Mount Olive
39° 4' 16.03" N
89° 44' 7.26" W

Missouri Blues
Missouri

Through the
Silverness of
Landlocked
Sea of trees
Lined by
Generous spread
And slide
Of subtle shade
Stretched
O'er vales and hills
Of modified
Shires
And the fine
Weather whiteness
Of floatcloud
Over viscous
River rippling
Reflecting hot
Missouri blues

As if
Order
Is to be
Restored
Can I hold
The thread
Of narrative
In this torrent
Of inspiration
Or so the story
Goes West

Missouri River, St Louis
38° 45' 51.63" N
90° 10' 18.18" W

Drive-In Theatre, Carthage
37° 10' 23.38" N
94° 22' 8.16" W

Magnolia Service Station, Texola
35° 13' 8.15" N
99° 59' 30.37" W

Oklahoma City: The Missing
Oklahoma

Mad melt
Molten emotion
Of landrush
Range marked
For plain claim
Or reclaim
Hardened
To bronze
Patina of art

The unsettled
Resettled

The glass
Towers
Over red
Wells Fargo office
Reflect on
Uncaptured
Fleeting cloudsky
Wide as
The prairie
Beyond

Oh so pretty
Again

At dusk
The glow of
Warm dignity
Lights
The audience
Of empty chairs
Remembering

I linger
A while
With them
But I know
I too
Must push on
Toward the setting sun

Oklahoma City
35° 28' 10.51" N
97° 31' 4.51" W

Ann's Chicken Fry House, Oklahoma City
35° 30' 40.03" N
97° 35' 35.08" W

Parker Drilling Rig, Elk City
35° 24' 40.93" N
99° 24' 12.79" W

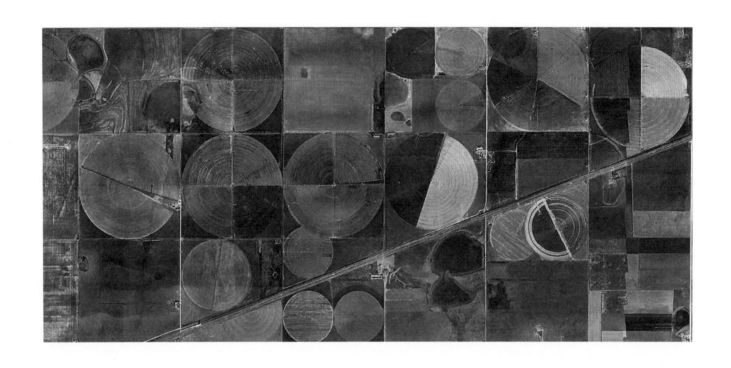

East of Amarillo
35° 19' 0.36" N
101° 27' 41.15" W

Paper Hat Antiques, Amarillo
35° 12' 40.07" N
101° 52' 38.68" W

Amarillo Coffee House
Texas

Amarillo
Is this the way
Now
Wasteland
Another lonely city
Seeming
Hollowed out

Seeking solace
In contrast
A flat white
Chic coffee house
Hopper tableau
Inside Out
As South Polk
Streetdusk
Falls desolate

I look out
On the negative
Image
And reflect on
What is inside

On a Texas
Tuesday morning
I head out
In the dawning
For the open
Plain
And the Cadillac
Ranch

Standing order

Amarillo Railway Yards
35° 11' 33.19" N
101° 49' 47.46" W

Billboards, Amarillo
35° 11' 35.24" N
101° 49' 40.35" W

Pink House, Amarillo
35° 11' 36.65" N
101° 49' 41.09" W

Cadillac Ranch
Amarillo, Texas

Pale prelude
To panhandle
Range opening
From Amarillo

Edgelands ranch
Where the Cadillac
Crop row grows
Incongruous
Slanted together
Marking time
Against some
Prairie wind
Of change
Implied
Echoes the route
Hard edged

Layers
Of sprayskin
Paint accrue
On metal totems
Of manhood
Individualising

Rolling change still
Distinguishing
The once distinctive

No grandeur
No natural spectacle
Just the land
Worked and walked on
Appreciated
By the closer at hand
Created and set
At classic angle
Constantly reworked
Always in the act
Of becoming
Abstract

What do they stand
For

Another road
To understanding
Apparently

Cadillac Ranch
35° 11' 16.68" N
101° 59' 14.87" W

Halfway
Adrian, Texas

Historic 66
Halfway is
High Plains
Prairie panhandle
Texas wide
And seeming empty

Eleven thirty-nine gone
The same to go
Marks the road
And those getting
The trip gather
To straddle the line
And pose with the sign
In Adrian

A tiny two diner
Old Route town
Off Interstate 40
At heart it
Stands for most

Fitting

I share a sense
Of having been somewhere
Of being somewhere
Of going somewhere
Mourning
Celebrating anticipating
Reflected inflected
Over coffee and
Home made pie
With welcome
Waitress warmth
How ya doin' Hon
Homely
A long way
From home

Thrown on
My own resources
I found
Plenty
I liked
When I wasn't looking

And I trade
My stories again

Midpoint Cafe, Adrian
35° 16' 14.63" N
102° 40' 23.40" W

Tucumari Trading Post
35° 10' 9.39" N
103° 44' 56.31" W

Blue Swallow Motel, Tucumari
35° 10' 18.71" N
103° 42' 58.63" W

Magnolia Service Station, Tucumari
35° 10' 17.90" N
103° 44' 18.63" W

Texaco Station, Tucumari
35° 10' 18.98" N
103° 42' 42.89" W

Lawrence, O'Keeffe And The Land Of Enchantment
New Mexico

Touch
The landscape
Lifechanging
Lawrence tree

Spaces and surfaces

High desert hills
O'Keeffe coloured
Roll charcoal black
Cottonwood ashgrey
Bleachbone white bluffs
Cliffs of coral
And cream
Mountains of lavender
And sage
Womanflowers
Of graphic power

Magnified
Ride revealing
Rio Grande
Skinclose
To red hills

A brilliant proud
New Mexico
Mountain state morning
Magnificent fierce
Appears
As if by magic
From thin air

Sunrise Snowies
Shine high
Saviours blood peaks

South East
Of Santa Fe
Skyblue
Break through
The looking
Glass enchantment
Shattering
Soul stilling
Savage pilgrimage

Wide open

All the old worlds
Give way
To the new

Outside in

Hello! Georgia -
It is September
And you are
Long past blue

The naming
Of emotion

Infamous green

Look for
The ribbon of
Road long past
The view

A studio model

Rio Grande, Albuquerque
35° 8' 47.08" N
106° 40' 39.05" W

Silence Shared With Nan Shepherd
New Mexico

Seeking silence
Shows how seldom
It can be found

When wind falls
No wind
Windsong

Sounding stills
Slip
Out of time

Soft September
Dawn draws
High desert plateau

The sensing world
Suspended
As light sensitive

Night
Stops
Its slide away

To a sky
Of light and colour
With rhyme

In rock
And sand
Run through hand

Crystal clear
Unhazed yet
Anticipating

White

Lean forward
To listen
Too

An image
Held
In a new
Element

Engagement
End of longing

Cottonwood Springs Trail, Albuquerque
35° 9' 49.61" N
106° 28' 9.49" W

Historic Route 66, Laguna Pueblo
35° 2' 18.52" N
107° 23' 19.08" W

Mission Church, Laguna Pueblo
35° 2' 4.42" N
107° 23' 20.47" W

Pueblo Style
Santa Fe, New Mexico

Where
Loop and Trail
Thread together
The oldest
Capital
High and dry
But never
Arid
Breathless beauty
Below the high
Sharp peaks
Of achievement

Beneath
Ultramarine
On the
Dancing ground
Of the sun
Ochre and umber
Earth re-imagined
And re-presented
Baked adobe
Burnt and raw

Sandyellow
Sits squat
Square
Round cornered
Earthclose
Pueblo style

A city
Different
Architecture
Of art and secrets
Hide and reveal
Absorb and release
What is material
Terroir for ideas
Nature thoughts
Intentions inspiration
Intellect to invention
It works
Pueblo style

Movements
Of millennia

Cultures captured
Concentrated
In courtyards
Plazas
Shadows umbral
Contrast
Secrets and art
World re-imagined
And represented
And always
The light
Pueblo style

I have
Found
My own way
Here
English strand
Stirred
Thread together
Pueblo style

Pueblo House, Santa Fe
35° 41' 8.30" N
105° 56' 12.67" W

Native American Maker
Santa Fe, New Mexico

In their wake
Liquid free and tender
Wild and loose
To your spirit

Heavy with memory
Your dark eyes
Deceived
By familiarity
Cast down
To your knowing hands
Cupped cradling
In your lap
Fingers intricate
Patterns unique
And recognised

Silence drawn
Slowly reluctantly
Unlacing untangling
Allowing the web
Of thoughts
To slip away
Cast off
Sighing

Dreamcatcher

Pick up
The threads
Again

Trading Post, Santa Fe
35° 41' 15.42" N
105° 56' 26.28" W

Casa Sena Courtyard Garden
Santa Fe, New Mexico

Unsuspected
From Sena Plaza
Secret
As Manhattan
Become half life
Meetings
Two doors down

Crowded green
Flower embroidered
Casa Sena
Adobe architected
Cooling
Courtyard garden
Incidentally planted
A fecund haven
Of humidity
In high and dry
Frowsy drowsy
Heat
Drawn up
Into thin air
By sun grade
Shade and shelter
From desert winds
Drawn in
By waterwarm
Conspiracy
Of scents

Shared with
Long ago
And far away
Suddenly drawn
Close
Led up
The bakebrick path
By turns

Hidden and revealed

Leafgreen
Flowersweet
Poignant beautiful
Earthy and desirable
To the roots
I share
Its fine
Carelessness

Just as linger
Tendrils
Tug and tempt
I know
I need
The road
Again
I get the trip

Sena Plaza, Santa Fe
35° 41' 15.63" N
105° 56' 9.64" W

Cirrocumulus Wander Lonely Over Interstate 25 At A Standstill
Albuquerque, New Mexico

Light static white
Noise on my
Car radio
Searching for
That singular station
Autodetuned
Above Albuquerque
Signal
Not to be found

Though it seems
All New Mexico
Is State Fair bound
To play out
Like Country
And Western songs
Come to life
In candy stripe

Santa Fe loop
Interstate 25
At a standstill
Windscreened

I have chance
To explore
A Weatherworld
Of airs and hours
The everchanging
Continent
Above a continent

Cloudland

Light moving white
Towers torn
To skyskein
Threads
Stories shreds
Told
Because they love
Windsought
Horizons too

Effervescent
The sounds of
AirPlayful

Cirrocumulus yearning
To kiss
At their edges
Boiling away
Hiss
Light static white

Cloudthought cover
Bluebreaking
Bliss of solitude
To the full
Stare of sun

Floating
Fairweather friends
Fizz
In company
But wandering still
Cloudscape and cars
Finally
Moving on

Interstate 25, Bernalillo
35° 27' 3.22" N
106° 21' 2.83" W

Relativity
Continental Divide, New Mexico

I wait at
Reds on 66
Railroad crossing
Figuring which
Wrong side
Of these tracks
I can be
On
A light bell
Tolls pulse quick

With steel purpose
Mile long train
Speedcrossing
Corndust and cobalt
Hauling freight

Blank sided
Boxcar frames
Shutter by
My ad hoc
Drive In
Unusually
Hiding scenes

A lonesome
Long horn dopplers
Changing its tone

Iconic
Laconic
Ironic
Calling for
The purple skies
Of mountain horizon
Going west

Waiting
Time for my
Train of thought
Never stands
Still

The second
Double engine
Concludes
This showing
I cross
The tracks
Catch the train
And cruise
Parallel paced
For miles

Iron road
Where they
Drove the spike

That drove down
The wagon train
And nailed
The cattle drive
In their time
The rutted way
West
National Old Trails
Paved and tracked
But not yet
Tamed

Time
A waster
Space
A cohort

My words
Are moving
Again
Too

I feel
Their gravity

Gallup, near Continental Divide
35° 31' 39.76" N
108° 44' 39.84" W

Headwater In Sand
Painted Desert, Arizona

By Tiponi and Tawa
Kachina and Chinde
Whipple Lacey and wash
66
Caught in colours
Dazzled by clarity

An abstract
Dream of sand

Love
Creates in us
What was lacking
Though yearning
We did not
Know the lack
Before it was
Satisfied
The headwater
Is that wellspring
That purely
Issues
The best of us
Parched

Earthcoloured
This work
This art
Is nothing
But working
Towards stillness
That opens
The possibility
Of rediscovery
Of the great
And simple
Images
In whose
Presence
Our hearts
First opened
Together

Whipple Point, Painted Desert
35° 4' 2.58" N
109° 47' 51.70" W

Painted Desert (1)
36° 31' 14.75" N
109° 20' 35.80" W

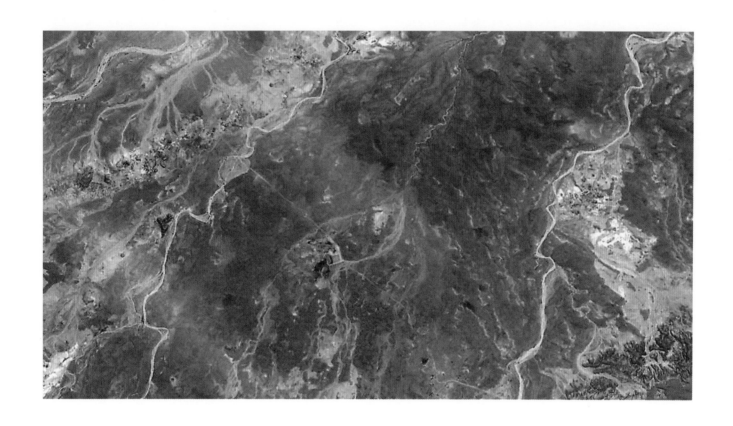

Painted Desert (2)
34° 58' 59.06" N
110° 26' 2.38" W

Petrified Forest
Arizona

Revealed
By era
Long erosion

Left in
Landscape
Tectonically raised and
Volcano buried
As arid
As it was
Once lush

Windworn and
Watered down
To dust

Aside
Unyielding mesas
Texture and tone
Of fossilised
Giant elephant
Carcases
With hardest
Hide

A still
Life of trees

Ageless
Composition

Disarticulated
Fallen
Body works
Bole butt and burr
Beautiful
As they were
In a life
Before
Speak of
Forests
Freed

Quartzed silica
Run through
With oxide traces
Washed in
Where
Sap and water
Once coursed

Crystalline colours
Cross section
Bark bound
Stone set record
Replacing
Windhistory
And stormstory
Heartwood
Showing only
Age beyond ages
Rings true

New wayleave
Through
What was
Wildwood
Jasper and Crystal
Forests
Across
Agate Bridge
I scan
The badlands
From
Blue Mesa
Fingertrace

The rockface
Petroglyphs
At Newspaper Rock

Narrators
Ancient and modern
Stories to tell
Stonespeak
Of journeys
Ways and means

Prospects place and progress

Later lodged
In the Holbrook
Globetrotter Motel
Touchstoned
I am inspired
To make marks
Of my own

More or less
Monumental

The Tepees, Petrified Forest
34° 56' 27.85" N
109° 46' 43.59" W

Polarised View

Holbrook, Winslow and Meteor Crater, Arizona

Even through
Wayfarers
Sun half closed
My eyes
Polarised
Globetrotter Lodge
Courtyard pool
Calls seductively
I see through her
Sultry slick
Sleepy sexy swim
Horizontality

Come on
You can have me
To yourself

Beadsweat
Trickled
I made
My excuses
And melted
Away for
Afternoon excursion
From Holbrook

Trusting in the magic
Of the off ramp

Off I40 West
Doubleback
For downtown
Winslow
Just to stand
On a corner
Where still
I hear
The sound of
My own wheels
And see my own
Seven women
In my mindeye
As the earworm runs
Unshakeable
Nothing more potent
Than popular song

Loadloosened
I run down
The Mother Road
For Meteor Crater

The climb
To the rim
Reveals
A big round hole
In the ground
A scientific still
Of molten heavenly
Stonesplash

Turning from
Prose and
Prosaic to poetry
I see landscape
Laid out in
Front of me
The real
Natural wonder
From the perfect
Meteor made
Viewpoint
It certainly
Knew what
It was doing

Senseful
Aimfully wandering
Highway to byway
I drive back
Through that view
To a Holbrook
Wigwam Motel
Sunset shared
Last touch to
Tops of tipis
Softening their
Concrete skins
Echoes quiet
Petrified Forest
Formations

The Globetrotter pool
Tired of waiting
And brazenly
Unfaithful

Unlike Sweetheart State

Wigwam Motel, Holbrook
34° 54' 9.80" N
110° 10' 9.33" W

Winslow
35° 1' 45.05" N
110° 42' 44.96" W

Flagstaff
35° 11' 32.42" N
111° 40' 2.89" W

Driving
Navajo Nation, Arizona and Utah

Driving
The Navajo Nation
From Chelly Canyon
To Monument Valley
Across Arizona
Clipping Utah

It is not pretty
But my word
It is beautiful
And burns
Its insistent way
Onto memory
Imagination
And by heart

Riding the road
Rolling ridges
Horizon to horizon
To Vanishing Point
Silver skylinings
Shining through
The play of light
Show and shadow
Sets aside
Even concrete highway
Designs on
Uniformity

Pulsing with longing
The tyres
Kerouac kerouac
Kerouac kerouac
The blacktop beat
Repeated
Until the words
Lose meaning
For new notes
Written without
Stops

Radio silence
Solo shoutsinging
An unaccompanied scatsong
Time signatured by
Broken yellow median

A non-routine routine
It's a driving
Rhythm
I inhabit
Day in
Day out
Without doubt

Near Round Rock
36° 31' 2.29" N
109° 29' 7.82" W

The View
Monument Valley, Arizona

September sunset
And sunrise
Across Monument Valley
Equinox aligned

My sense
My feeling
Set and climb
With the light
Even
As day
And night

I have put myself
In the way of beauty
Magnetised
Mesmerised
By
The View

Every iconic
Evolutionary mesa
Butte and stack
Each characterful
Eminence
More than
More of the same
More than can
Be taken in
At first sight
Or single sweep

Unearthered
Solitary strange and sensitive
Together gathered
Exposed
Against a landscape
Where the backdrop
Blue of distance
Becomes visible
Beyond
Beneath lazuli
Skies
Shot with
White and gold

Desolate
Windworn
Waterborn
Terracottta
Shale and sandstone
Market for inspiration
Ideas and imagination
Flawlessness
Freely traded

Unshod
Palomino hooves
Paw the ground
Fine dust
Stirred
Falls like
Particles
Of sunlight

Slowly dying
To the valley
Floor
Paused

A timeless space
For the gravity
Of emotion
Lightness of being
And enveloping
Light and
Crucible
Condensing sun
Through
Umbral charcoal
To dark and
Star full heavens
Storm
Of infinite beauty

Formations
So absolute
There is
No perspective
On them

But them

No tolerance
For synonym
But enchanted
By naming

And images
Precise and
Particular
Clarity allegiance and intimacy

The borders
Of myth
Legend and fact
Here
Are not decisive

Dream knowable
Relayed by ancients
Would be
Visionaries and interpreters
Replayed
By auteurs

Bloodgold dawn
Makes an entrance
Spirits rise
With the sun

I draw in
The day
Great draughts
Of space time
Light and land
As I fill
I feel
My capacity grow

The View Hotel, Monument Valley
36° 58' 54.32" N
110° 6' 45.22" W

On Feeling At Home Somewhere You've Never Been

John Ford Point, Monument Valley, Arizona

Delicate
But potent

More than
A twinge
In the heart
Made from another
Memory
Of movie images
However iconic
The finest
Screenplay
Never written

Not that thing
Some are
Too pleased
To call
Déjà vu

But
Sometime
In some
Special place

I catch myself
From the corner
Of my eye
A fleeting glimpse

My impression
Is of a half smile
Of recognition

I see
John Ford's
Point now

And I sense
Companionship

A fellow
Feeling

Resonant

Of the moment
Great moment

Given back
What I brought
Clearly

A human
Being
Doing
A man
Journeying

There

Understood
Naturally

Confronted
By the reality
That is
Of the mind
And heart

It is where
The home
Is

Monument Valley
36° 58' 43.92" N
110° 11' 3.00" W

Raising Arizona
Arizona

Limb looseningly lyric
Bitter sweet
Irresistible inescapable
Music of my heart
Muse
The daughter of memory
Songs of the
High dry
Land
Rock and sand
Where performance
Is rooted
Still
There to be read
If I slow
My looking
And heard
In the winds
Undersong
If I still
My own noise

Give me seven
More senses
Than the seven
I have
To engage
My world
Inside and out
And there would
Still
Be sensations
To suck up
And savour
With new parts
Of me
To satisfy
Beyond
This experience

Sing to me
I yearn
For wonders
Will never cease

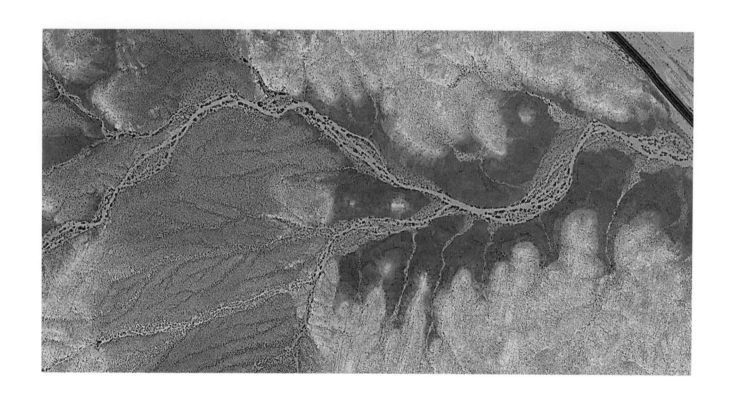

Desert View Drive
35° 51' 57.65" N
111° 29' 16.43" W

Grand Canyon
Arizona

I get sublime
I get awesome
But
In search of awe
I walked the
Paths
Along and down
From El Tovar
And come up
Dry
And decide
To sleep on it

The morning after
I'm driving
The South Rim

Time after time
I stepped out
Into too much
To take in
And not enough

Cutting Colorado
Rolling deep and rapid
Like a poem
Finished before
I understand it
Surviving

In the valley
Of its making

Actor
Of transformation
Fiction friction

Now edited
It is
No longer
Interesting me

It is
What it is
Exactly
What it is
Named
Is all
That beautiful barrier narrative
Set in stone
Must accept image
Jealously
Self-curated

But look
I was not touched
It is no wonder
That earth did not move
For me

Maybe I was on
The besotted rebound
From Monument Valley
There is nothing
For it
But to put it
Behind me

Lone tree rooted in rock
Objects
In the mirror are closer than they appear

Losing touch
I show it
My tail lights
And press on

Inverted skycanyons
Rolling blueblack below
Towering thunderheads
Turbulent indigo
Threaten to bruise
The bullied sky
But they too
Keep their distance
Not their promise
No more than
Radar rumour
Of a Weather
Channel worry

Clear eyed and skies
Come up dry only I
Roll into Williams
And Seligman
Street scenes

Of more recent
History roadmade
Rhymed if not
Repeated as both
Tragedy and farce
Huddled together
For survival

A different perspective

Grand Canyon
36° 4' 0.18" N
112° 8' 41.74" W

Pavement Ends, Seligman
35° 19' 51.46" N
112° 53' 0.83" W

Oatman
35° 1' 38.88" N
114° 23' 3.39" W

Nevada Blue Transmission

Lake Mead and the Mojave Desert, Nevada

The physics of
A clear cold
Dream
Blue eyed day
Light
Sky geometry
Gliding on
Guiding principles
Lighting lucid as
A theorem
Deliberate as
A strategem
For outwitting
Wily nights wild nature

Muddy and River
Ranges rockrising
With heat action
Dust devils dance
Mute asides to
Desert dialogue
With Boldered
Colarado
Run from snow melt
Whiterush to stillblue

Mead madewater
Potable for pleasure
And power
Broken from roar
To whisper

Roll to ride
Reinforced and rock
Constructivist collide
To contain surfaces
Bound cubist
Lakecapes
Analytic to synthetic
Coldwater perspective
Fault forced faces
And hot plains planes

Rising skyward
Sun driven airs
Water
In all its states
Through
The blue transmission
Powering probabilities

Lake Mead
36° 1' 30.31" N
114° 47' 53.84" W

Las Vegas
36° 10' 35.53" N
115° 0' 37.32" W

EZ Pawn, Las Vegas
36° 10' 3.05" N
115° 8' 30.69" W

Vegas
Las Vegas, Nevada

Kitsch and culture
Fries and fine
Dining
Aircon chill and
Burning strip
Daylight and daynight
Huge inside
Reduced outside
Rational and rash

What more
Can I tell you
About Vegas

Except
A little
Light headed at
Last leg looming
It was where
I cashed in
The faithful
Grey SUV

My prairie rolling
Forest forging
Canyon crawling
Covered wagon
And put it all
On red

The colour
Of Lady Luck
Lipstick and Louboutins
Cliché but not cheap
A carmine
Chevy Camaro
Convertible
And the top down
High rolling
Desert scorch
Dragging Main
To California

Says it all
Really

New York - New York Hotel and Casino, Las Vegas
36° 6' 5.11" N
115° 10' 25.48" W

What I Think About When I Think About Driving Desert Night With The Ragtop Down
Mojave Desert, Nevada and California

I am opened
To nightsky
Astonished
And astonishing

Mojave moon
On September
Sweetwater sky
Slim crescent
Reclining
Like a bright clef
Beginning
Curved staves
Of the infinite
On which stars note
Their song
Endless pouring pure
Loving the dark
Blue silences
Between

Mojave moon
On September
Sweetwater sky
Shining clear
As silver images
Placed by purpose
On the surface
Of mirage pool
Of cool reflection

Mojave moon
On September
Sweetwater sky
Broken arc
From perfect round
Like things
That are and aren't
The lie of the land
Eyetricks and truth
Holding image

A deep field
Silvergreyed silence
Exchanging dreams

Mojave moon
On September
Sweetwater sky
Heavy lidded
With her night work
Lazy anguishing breeze
Caresses
Chill sands and
Unscrolls
The last of night
Unlocks dark doors
To drive on dawn
And articulates day

Mojave Desert
34° 43' 26.10" N
115° 57' 32.64" W

Needles Freeway
34° 43' 34.79" N
115° 36' 20.07" W

Motel, Twentynine Palms
34° 7' 54.29" N
116° 3' 41.94" W

Coffee Caramel Glacier
Santa Barbara, California

Skirted Santa Monica
Passed Pasadena
Hot Hollywood
By Beverley Hills
Over Malibu
Ventura Highway highs

The Mother Road
Finally
Slips off
Her highway
State of Mind
Kinda shoes
And sinks
Her tired toes
Into West Coast
Sand letting
Sea suck
Sixty-Six to
History
And my stories
Traded
open road for promiseland

Santa Barbara
Hotsweet and cool
Coffee caramel
Glacier
Pure pleasure
I loved its
Slid riviera
From Mission
And Santa Ynez
To Pacific

Evening sun
On my face
Slides slowly
Into sea
I fingerscribe
A heart
In the wet sand
Making an impression
In the way
I want
The word

Pelicans on
Stearns Wharf Pier
Palm lined
Avenues
And terracotta
Pantiled roofscape
Mellowed

At State and Mission
McConnell's
Blended me
Bespoke icecream
Hotsweet and cool
Coffee caramel
Glacier
Pure pleasure
I loved it

Santa Barbara
34° 24' 41.07" N
119° 41' 16.89" W

The English Garden, Simpson House Inn – The Veranda

Santa Barbara, California

Embodying warmth
Wit and welcome
The Inn veranda
Whitewrapping
In genteel embrace
Comfort and charm
A place to sit
To sup and see
To contemplate
Word and world
To picture home
And northland

Start the day
A whole colour box
Thrown Art
Fully on
Gardenscape ground
Draped in tissued mist
The sun rises through

Crisp cloth
Breakfast table
Pinpoint a pleasure
Isolate a feeling

Fix on its
Salts and nectars
Hot liquids stir
Uncurl unhurried
Swirl in and out
Of focus
Cream in coffee

Daythreads spread
Beyond
Screenleaf trees
Breezegreen forms
Shrubs surround
To take in
Seaplants succulent
Fruit and flowerfade
Reveal light and shade
Last flush of foodplants
Fountain played
Sotto soundscape
Ambience sparkling

Sprinklerspritzed
September lawns hissing
A wistful song

Of midsummer long
And springfresh green

Sea tang sky
Sussurus and cloud
Seep together
Rundrip with colour
Opal blood
Fig ripening
Grain rinsed
Eggshell blue
The evening slowgold
And longshadowed

At last dusky musky
Shaded weatherboard hoards
Set apart scents
Released by the heat
And the humid relaxes
Into smudged charcoal
Atmospheres rounded
With indefinite line
And the veranda lamps
Bring things close
Into the warmfold

With the deepening
Mystery beyond

Fall into indigo
Deep as lining
A gem case
Gold leaf coffered for
Vaulting jewelstar light
Rising into midnight blue
Renewed infinity sighing

Trading my stories
The moment will come
Concentrated spread
Over a day
A poem resolved
Over its given time

I simply
Raise my eyemind
For the next horizon

In ruthless search
Of my next theme.

East Cabrillo Boulevard, Santa Barbara
34° 25' 10.00" N
119° 39' 43.80" W

Coda: Both Sides Now
Route 66, USA

For a continent
Originated in
Stone wood water weather
Mediated through
Ecology politics culture economics
Invented by
Direction destination pursuit dream

Essentially greatest
Whitman poem
Still being
Developed

Truth makes myth
Myth makes myth
Myth makes truth
More or less
Agreed on

Coastculture
Fuelled by still
Deep and true
Vernacular stories
Of the quiet
Centre

For me
Imagination and experience
Road trip and romance
All
In the balance
Assaying Americana
In the lee
Of Labor Day
Downstream of downturn

Reading the land
State lines
States of mind
Sites and situations
Stories of contrasts
Continuity and change
Time to time
open road
for promiseland

The many
Routes of 66
Escaping definition
Self-evidently sought
Claimed but never
Caught

Figurative
And figurative
Mediated
By the merry
Go round
Of memory
Revelation
And anticipation
Spinning
Storytrading tale
At once
Art's lietruth and
Aimed for beauty

John and Jack
Magnificent and mundane
Monstrous and moving
Pastiche and penetrating
Monumental and modest
Histrionic and heartfelt
Hubris and humility
Sensual and savage
Closeness and chasms
Divides and rules
Rich and ragged
Poverty and plenty

Push and pull
Passionate and precise
Prosaic and poetic
promiseland and plot lost
Presentcity and Pasttown
Me and we
Continent and community
Nation and neighbourhood
Foreign and familiar
One State and the next
One state and another
United and untied
Time zones and timeless
Energy and extremes
Ideas and frontiers
Restless and rooted
Change and curation
Mother Road and Main Street USA

Welcome welcoming and wonder full.

Mural, Seligman
35° 19' 37.00" N
112° 52' 30.91" W

Route 66 – A Brief History

The road trip is an enduring symbol of Americana and US Route 66 from Chicago, Illinois to the California coast is the most iconic of these.

Prefigured by westbound wagon and railroad routes, National Old Trails and State roads, Route 66 was established on November 11, 1926.

Becoming known as 'The Mother Road' Route 66 was part of the original US Highway System and soon claimed its place as, arguably, the most famous road in America and then worldwide.

US 66 served as a major path for those who migrated west during the depression dust bowl of the 1930s – realised in John Steinbeck's 1939 Pullitzer prizewinning novel 'The Grapes Of Wrath' and its John Ford 1940 Hollywood film interpretation.

A fixture in popular culture, the road continued to inspire and feature in many other books and articles, music and movies and in visual art.

Its legend and myth persisted through removal of the Route 66 designation from the National Highway System and replacement by new Interstate Highways.

It is now being re-interpreted through historical rediscovery, 'get your kicks' tourism and, still, through art.

Traversing the landscape of a continent in all its magnificent diversity, the journey also rewards by revealing the energy of an ever-changing America and Americana, including the engaging eccentricities of Route 66 road trip memorabilia along the way.

Planning, enjoying and capturing that experience continues to challenge and excite travellers and artists alike.